THE TRAGEDY OF 1662

THE EJECTION AND PERSECUTION OF THE PURITANS

BY LEE GATISS

The Latimer Trust

ISBN 0-946307-60-1

EAN   9780946307609

Published by the Latimer Trust

PO Box 26685

London N14 4XQ

www.latimertrust.org

CONTENTS

Introduction

In these days of spiritual ignorance in the country and doctrinal laxity in the church, many Anglicans look back to former times with a certain degree of wistfulness. Declining electoral rolls speak of a nation less focused on the things of God than seems to have been the case in centuries gone by when our ancient and airy church buildings must, we conjecture, have pulsated with activity and vibrancy. In a period of liturgical diversity and confusion, others feel the disappearance of a uniform standard of worship across the denomination to be an incalculable injury, particularly as it permits both an unfitting lack of gravity in church services and the propagation of dubious theology. In an era of polarisation in ecclesiastical politics with pressure groups and 'turbulent priests' disturbing the peace of the church, the search for authoritative leadership to impose order on a fractious, wayward communion is an understandable desire.

One date lingers in the collective Anglican memory as suggestive of a golden era: 1662. Were not churches full in the seventeenth century? Were not the Thirty-nine Articles chiselled into every *Book of Common Prayer* and subscribed to *ex animo* by the clergy? Did not that same book, hallowed by over a century of sacred use, ensure unity and uniformity in the public meetings of every English parish, with a reverent dignity and stylistic polish often wanting in modern expressions of church? Those were the days when bishops were bishops and were not afraid to excommunicate heretics and bring discipline to bear on those of notorious, scandalous life!

Yet 1662 was not a good year for those to whom the

gospel and a good conscience were more precious than the institutional church. The soft-focus lens of forgetfulness has blurred the historical picture, and the shifting sands of the religious scene have deceived many into an unfounded confidence in and a too easy ownership of that Restoration settlement. There may indeed be many excellent things to learn from it. But this study will examine the tragedy of 1662, and the way in which 'evangelical' puritans were excluded from and then persecuted by the established Church of England.

1.   Part One: The Great Ejection

1.1.   Background: From Reformation to Civil War

The English Reformation had broken the stranglehold of Rome and begun a long process of social and religious change. This inevitably brought tensions in the church between the forces of conservatism, seeking to retain the structures and theologies of the past, and the forces of transformation which sought to change the English church in various, supposedly biblical, directions. This tension played itself out at the highest level as the government lurched from side to side during the reigns of Protestant Edward (1547-53) and Roman Catholic Mary (1553-58). The religious scene of 1558-1603 is often portrayed as the Elizabethan 'Settlement', a stable *via media* between Rome and Geneva, and yet there remained significant tensions beneath the surface which meant it was never a very comfortable settlement.

The early seventeenth century saw continued efforts at reform and reaction; these, combined with other political and economic factors, had spilled over into Civil War. The failure of the Cromwells to achieve a satisfying peace by abolishing the crown and suppressing the episcopalian Church of England with its Prayer Book had led, eventually, to calls for the return of the monarchy. So, as A. G. Matthews succinctly puts it:

> The problem of Puritanism which faced the statesmen of the Restoration was no new one; for a century past it had with varying intensity vexed the peace of church and state. The attempt of Charles I to solve it by persecution had resulted in the Civil War; the attempt of the Parliament to solve it by a counter-persecution had brought about the King's return. And now in 1660, after all these years of troubled experience, the question once more presented itself as the question of the day – what was to be done with the Puritans?[1]

By the seventeenth century, as Richard Baxter says, 'Any Man that was for a Spiritual serious way of Worship (though he were for moderate Episcopacy and Liturgy), and that lived according to his Profession, was called commonly a Presbyterian, as formerly he was called a Puritan, unless he joined himself to Independents, Anabaptists, or some other Sect which might afford him a more odious Name'.[2] The problem with these 'presbyterians', as one seventeenth century poet depicting the puritans humorously wrote, was that they ...

---

[1] A. G. Matthews, *Calamy Revised: Being a Revision of Edmund Calamy's Account of the Ministers and Others Ejected and Silenced, 1660-1662* (Oxford: Clarendon Press, 1988 [1934]) p. ix.

[2] See *Reliquiae Baxterianae* (London: Matthew Sylvester, 1696), Part II, p. 278. I am very grateful to Wendy Bell, Librarian of Oak Hill College for allowing me extended access to the 1696 edition of Baxter's autobiography from the Latimer Collection. For more on *Reliquiae Baxterianae*, see my article "The Autobiography of a 'Meer Christian': Richard Baxter's Account of the Restoration" on *The Theologian* (www.theologian.org.uk).

Call fire and sword and desolation,
A godly thorough reformation,
Which always must be carried on,
And still be doing, never done;
As if religion were intended
For nothing else but to be mended.
A sect, whose chief devotion lies
In odd perverse antipathies;
In falling out with that or this,
And finding somewhat still amiss.[3]

This popular characterisation fails to appreciate of course that the picture could equally well be drawn the other way around. Why should it be the reforming 'modernising' puritans who are cast as the problem, and not rather the innately conservative and reactionary forces which sought to resist the reformed doctrine of *Ecclesia Reformata Semper Reformanda*?[4] The puritans were convinced that the church could not rest on its laurels or fall backwards into mediaeval superstition or Roman Catholicism. Their attitude of constant vigilance would quickly come into conflict with the intransigent new regime which sought not only to rebuild the old system of monarchy and established church but also to alienate those they held responsible for the new king's former exile.

1.2. *The Restoration of Charles II*

Charles II himself was concerned above all never to go travelling again: not only to keep his head (unlike his father)

---

[3] From *Hudibras* (First Part, Canto I, lines 187-216) by Samuel Butler (1613-1680) written sometime in 1660-1680. See C. Ricks (ed.), *The Oxford Book of English Verse* (Oxford: OUP, 1999), p. 227.
[4] The reformed church is always being reformed.

but to reign and die on his throne. His Declaration from Breda in the Netherlands before re-entering the country had promised 'a liberty to tender consciences; and that no man shall be disquieted, or called in question, for differences of opinion in matters of religion which do not disturb the peace of the kingdom.'[5] This was greeted with delighted optimism. When he returned to the country, 'as he past through the City towards Westminster, the London ministers in their Places attended him with Acclamations, and by the hands of old Mr Arthur Jackson, presented him with a Rich-adorned Bible, which he received, and told them it should be the Rule of his Actions.'[6] It seemed as if the so-called 'presbyterians', the Calvinistic puritans committed to the Bible and a national church structure, would have their way.

Richard Baxter and other leading puritan divines were appointed chaplains to the king and granted an audience with him.[7] At Breda, puritan representatives had stressed that although they were not enemies of a moderate form of episcopacy, they were concerned that the *Book of Common Prayer* would be re-introduced in the royal chapel, along with the surplice and ceremonies to which they objected. According to Clarendon, Charles himself replied 'with some warmth, that whilst he gave them liberty, he would not have his own taken from him; that he had always used that form of service, which he thought the best in the world... [T]hey were

---

[5] *Declaration of King Charles II from Breda* from Clarendon's *History of the Rebellion* Book xvi, §§ 193-7 (Oxford 1849), vol. vi, pp. 232-234 as reprinted in G. Gould, *Documents Relating to the Settlement of the Church of England by the Act of Uniformity of 1662* (London: W. Kent & Co, 1862), p. 3.
[6] *Reliquiae Baxterianae*, Part II, p. 218. cf. p. 144 of R. Baxter, *The Autobiography of Richard Baxter* abridged by J. M. Lloyd Thomas, edited with an introduction by N. H. Keeble (London: J. M. Dent & Sons, 1985).
[7] Baxter, *Reliquiae Baxterianae*, Part II, p. 229.

very much unsatisfied with him, whom they thought to have found more flexible.'[8] Yet Baxter's account of the discussions they had with the king once he was back in London is more positive and hopeful. At hearing of Charles's zeal to search for peaceful compromise between the religious parties he records that 'old Mr Ash burst out into Tears with Joy and could not forbear expressing what Gladness this Promise of his Majesty had put into his heart.'[9]

His heart, however, would soon be broken. All was not as it appeared behind the scenes. 'It seems that the king himself was sincere enough in his statements,' writes Gerald Bray, 'but he was surrounded by men who were thirsting for revenge. Once he was safely back on the throne, Charles found that he had to make concessions to these extremists, and the good intentions of Breda were seriously compromised as a result.'[10] In 1660 the country was unprepared for the immediate restoration of episcopacy as well as monarchy; most anticipated that there would be liberty, toleration, and a new settlement to be negotiated and debated by Parliament in due course. For some months the king, his advisors, and the episcopalian leaders paid lip service to this general expectation. At the same time they proceeded quietly and cautiously to recapture the establishment by stealth. So while '[t]he King might speak graciously to his Presbyterian subjects ... his favour was

---

[8] *Interview of the Presbyterian Ministers with King Charles II at Breda* in Clarendon's *History of the Rebellion*, Book xvi, §§ 242-4, (Oxford, 1849), vol. vi, pp. 261-263 as reprinted in Gould, *Documents*, p. 5.
[9] *Reliquiae Baxterianae*, Part II, p. 231.
[10] G. Bray, *Documents of the English Reformation* (Cambridge: James Clarke & Co., 1994), p. 544.

showered on the Laudians.'[11]

In Ireland where Parliament was suspended and there was little need to negotiate with the puritans, they were quickly repressed and the old Church firmly restored. In England it happened more insidiously: petitions in favour of episcopacy and Prayer Book were organised in many English counties by the country gentry, probably at the instigation of the Court, with the effect that one contemporary commented, '[t]he generality of people are doting after prelacy and the Service-Book'.[12] At the same time, a standing committee of episcopal divines led by the Bishop of London used the Crown's patronage to appoint its members to strategic posts in both the Church and Universities.[13]

In less than two years both old Mr Ash, who cried for joy at the king's apparent desire for compromise, and old Mr Jackson, who gave the king a Bible, would be cast out of the

---

[11] R. S. Bosher, *The Making of the Restoration Settlement: The Influence of the Laudians 1649-1662* (London: Dacre Press, 1951), p. 155. The 'Laudians' here are so named for Archbishop Laud (1573-1645), a fervent opponent of earlier puritans. On 'Anglican' as a later, nineteenth century term to denote the episcopalian interest in this period see C. Podmore, *Aspects of Anglican Identity* (London: Church House Publishing, 2005), pp. 35-36. Aware of the anachronism, I will use it interchangeably with episcopalian.

[12] Sharp, quoted in Bosher, *Restoration Settlement*, p. 156.

[13] See Bosher's highly suggestive evidence for this in *Restoration Settlement*, pp. 159-161 which I. M. Green, *The Re-Establishment of the Church of England 1660-1663* (Oxford: OUP, 1978), p. 24 contests, claiming particularly that 'Episcopal government was not functioning fully in May 1661'. This may be so in many places, and not surprising given the lack of experienced diocesan administrators (Green, chapter VI *passim*); but Bosher's detailed work is at the very least highly suggestive of a resurgent Anglican attempt to influence things in their direction, and in London at least the Bishop was active in seeking to further a Laudian agenda from 1660 as we will see below. Green's own evidence points to a functioning and authority-wielding episcopacy early on (see his discussion on pp. 129-131).

church along with most of their fellow puritans.[14] This catastrophic event was foreshadowed in 1660 by the Act for Confirming and Restoring of Ministers which was a curious mixture of puritan and episcopalian concerns.[15] Apart from a requirement to take the oaths of allegiance and supremacy,[16] this imposed only one doctrinal test on those wishing to minister in the established church – requiring them to believe in infant baptism – and explicitly did not insist on episcopal ordination as a prerequisite to ecclesiastical office. It did, however, restore to their livings the clergy who had been removed during the 1640s and 50s. By this time at least fifty Congregationalist ministers had already withdrawn voluntarily from the vicarages they had occupied during the Republic.[17] A. G. Matthews calculates that the 1660 Act led to the ejection of a total of 695 mostly puritan ministers from their churches and the reinstallation of staunchly loyal old church Anglicans.[18] Since the Act was not intended permanently to alienate any but Anabaptists many thus ejected were able to find other livings, for the time being.[19]

---

[14] On Arthur Jackson, former President of Sion College and Rector of St Faith's in London see *Calamy Revised*, p. 290. I presume that 'old Mr Ash' who accompanied Baxter to see the king is Simeon Ashe '[o]ne of the leading London Presbyterian ministers' and Rector of St Austin's, London who 'went seasonably to Heaven at the very Time when he was cast out of the Church. He was bury'd the very Even of Bartholomew-Day' (*Calamy Revised*, p. 16).

[15] As Bosher helpfully notes in *Restoration Settlement*, p. 179, adding that it should be regarded as 'a Presbyterian measure making certain concessions to Anglicans, rather than *vice-versa.*'

[16] As noted by Gould in *Documents*, p. 26 footnote 1.

[17] M. Watts, *The Dissenters: From the Reformation to the French Revolution* (Oxford: Clarendon Press, 1978), p. 217.

[18] A. G. Matthews, *Calamy Revised*, pp. xii-xiii.

[19] Matthews calculates that 59 ministers ejected in 1660 were able to find other livings, only to fall foul of the Act of Uniformity two years later.

1.3. The Effect in London

London was uniquely turbulent and 'concentrated all the religious diversity that England possessed into a tiny space.'[20] It had the greatest concentration of nonconformists and nonconformist leaders in the country and more ministers were ejected here than in any other diocese. So it is a useful place in which to pause in order to add a local and personal colour to the story.[21] Among the ejected of 1660 were Samuel Wills, Rector of Birmingham and former Vicar of St Helen's, Bishopsgate (1644-7) who although the Court of Arches had declared in his favour was dispossessed by an apothecary called Slater 'partly by Fraud, and more by force'. Being of a peaceful disposition he decided not to contest this but preached instead in a chapel at the other end of town. He was later chased out of the county by a malicious prosecution.[22] Other ejected ministers in 1660 included 'a Man of great ability, and readiness' called Thomas Woodcock who was Rector of St Andrew, Undershaft,[23] and congregationalist Arminian, Tobias Conyers (Rector of St Ethelberga, Bishopsgate).[24] The former Rector of St Ethelberga, Edward Archer, found himself having to give way in his new Oxfordshire post to the former vicar who was one

---

[20] See P. Seaward, 'Gilbert Sheldon, the London Vestries, and the Defence of the Church' in T. Harris, P. Seaward, and M. Goldie (eds.), *The Politics of Religion in Restoration England* (Oxford: Basil Blackwell, 1990), p. 51.

[21] As will become apparent, I also have a personal interest in presenting the history of what is now the united benefice of St Helen, Bishopsgate with St Andrew, Undershaft & St Ethelburga, Bishopsgate & St Martin, Outwich & St Mary Axe, a benefice held in plurality with St Peter's, Cornhill by the Revd. William Taylor and where I myself served as Associate Minister while writing this study.

[22] *Calamy Revised*, p. 534.

[23] *Calamy Revised*, p. 543. The quote concerning his character comes from *Reliquiae Baxterianae*, Part III, p. 94.

[24] *ibid.*, p. 132.

Gilbert Sheldon, Bishop of London from 1660-63, later Archbishop of Canterbury, and one of the prime architects of the Restoration Settlement.[25]

Sheldon was a royalist Anglican of the first rank. He had spent time in prison during the 1640s by order of Parliament, was intimate with Royalist leaders during the Civil War, had ministered to Charles I in captivity and collected funds for Charles II during his exile.[26] As Cragg notes in his history of the Church of England in this period, 'Sheldon was an ecclesiastic, not a theologian, but he attacked every manifestation of Calvinism, whether in Church or State, in doctrine or polity.'[27] Not only was Sheldon keen to regain control of at least one of his former livings, but as Bishop of London he was charged with re-imposing order and uniformity on a diverse and radicalised Diocese. He was not afraid of using strong-arm tactics to achieve this end: he and his supporters regarded changing the governing constitutions of churches as one of the most useful tools for 'digging out the roots of nonconformity' and seem sometimes to have paid little attention to the wishes of even friendly parish elites.[28] Evidence of such an attack on

---

[25] *ibid.*, p. 14. Also ejected in 1660 were Edmund Brome, a former lecturer at St Peter's, Cornhill; Thomas Singleton, headmaster of Eton College (1655-60) and Reading School (1660), one time master of a school in St Mary Axe; and Thomas Underwood who worked alongside Woodcock at St Andrew, Undershaft (*Calamy Revised*, pp. 77, 444, 500).

[26] See Green, *The Re-Establishment of the Church of England*, pp. 93-94. See also A. G. Matthews, *Walker Revised: Being a revision of John Walker's Sufferings of the Clergy during the Grand Rebellion 1642-1660* (Oxford: Clarendon Press, 1988 [1948]), p. 76.

[27] G. R. Cragg, *From Puritanism to the Age of Reason: A Study of Changes in Religious Thought within the Church of England 1660 to 1700* (Cambridge: CUP, 1966), p. 22.

[28] Seaward, 'Gilbert Sheldon, the London Vestries', p. 57.

entrenched nonconformity comes from 'one of the most notoriously radical of city parishes, St Stephen's, Coleman Street' which was known even before the war for its 'strongly puritan flavour'[29] and was run by a former St Peter's, Cornhill lecturer called William Taylor.

Taylor ran the church through a series of committees nominally appointed by an open meeting of all the parishioners called a 'general vestry'. Since St Stephen's also had the right to appoint its own minister, the vestry and committees had immense influence. When the living was declared officially vacant due to the requirements of the 1660 Act, a meeting of the whole parish immediately re-elected Taylor and sparked a battle for control. The Bishop pressurised Taylor, but when the latter died in September 1661 (perhaps, as Seaward suggests, from exhaustion with the controversy) the parish appointed one man as his replacement while Sheldon appointed another. 'The parishioners had one important weapon, though, against the bishop,' writes Seaward. 'A large part of the minister's stipend had been customarily made up by the parish, its ancient endowment being inadequate. They now withheld it.'[30]

At this point, the Bishop and his allies in the parish attempted to change the constitution of the church to a 'select vestry' which could be more tightly controlled by a small group of people. This set in motion prolonged legal wrangling in which the church was advised by former Commonwealth statesman and lawyer, Bulstrode Whitelocke, a resident of the parish. Whitelocke often gave free legal

----

[29] *ibid.*, p. 61.
[30] *ibid.*, p. 63.

advice to presbyterian and congregationalist ministers, as well as parishioners in trouble for not attending worship, and even people he himself admitted were 'fanatics'. He was already involved in another defence against Sheldon's attack on churches in London: 'Early in 1661 he recorded in his diary how the parishioners of St Helen's, Bishopsgate had come to him for advice 'about a commission under the bishop's seal, appointing certain parishioners whom the bishop pleased to be the vestry of the parish.'"[31] In other words, what the Bishop tried against William Taylor's church he was also trying against St Helen's, Bishopsgate; that is, attempting to alter the constitution of the church so he could foist his own list of candidates onto a smaller, more select and compliant church council. In at least one parish (St Dunstan-in-the-West, Fleet Street) he did manage to remove 'some of the most troublesome radicals' and there is evidence of this tactic being used in at least a dozen other London churches.[32]

1.4. Settlement Negotiations

While Sheldon was busy in London and other returning episcopalians were working as hard as they could behind the scenes to re-establish themselves, negotiations continued for

---

[31] *ibid.*, p. 62. Sadly, as footnote 73 there records, 'No instrument exists in the vicar-general's book for this parish: nor do the vestry minutes survive.' Indeed, J. E. Cox (ed.), *The Annals of St Helen's Bishopsgate London* (London: Tinsley Brothers, 1876), p. 107 records a frustrating lacuna in the minutes between 1578 and 1676. The minutes for 1678 and 1694, however (pp. 108 and 111) do indicate that it was usual for the parish to themselves recommend and choose a man to be their Minister by election.

[32] *ibid.*, p. 68. For the numbers, see p. 54. St Helen's is not listed in the vicar-general's book (as noted above) along with the other 13 'instruments' for creating closed vestries, so we may surmise that other 'faculties' to ensure conformity were probably attempted and similarly not recorded.

a religious settlement. From July to October 1660 presbyterian divines, led by Calamy and Reynolds, drew up detailed proposals for the king's consideration, and were answered by the bishops. Baxter's abstract of the larger papers[33] provides an insight into the state of negotiations. They took for granted, they said, firm agreement in 'the doctrinal truths of the reformed religion'[34] but identified points of divergence on church government and discipline, liturgy, and ceremony.

On issues of polity they were in favour of Archbishop Usher's 'Reduced Episcopacy'. This was described as 'the true ancient primitive episcopacy or presidency as it was balanced and managed by a due commixtion of presbyters therewith, as a means to avoid corruptions, partiality, tyranny, and other evils which may be incident to the administration of one single person'.[35] This model called for smaller dioceses and more bishops (akin to the number of area/rural deans), acting in concert with authoritative synods at national, provincial, and deanery level. Concerning the liturgy, they distanced themselves from those such as John Owen who were against liturgies *per se*,[36] asserting that they were lawful if agreeable to the Bible, neither too tedious or too terse, of similar nature to other Reformed liturgies, not too rigorously imposed, and made allowance for the

---

[33] Submitted 'lest the reading of the larger should seem tedious to the king' (*Reliquiae Baxterianae,* Part II, p. 232).

[34] *Reliquiae Baxterianae,* Part II, p. 233.

[35] *Reliquiae Baxterianae,* Part II, p. 233-4. On p. 241 he admits that they did not all like Usher's model but 'it was the best [for] which we could have the least hope.' Usher's *Model of Church Government* can be found in *Reliquiae Baxterianae,* Part II, pp. 238-241 and Gould, *Documents,* pp. 22-26.

[36] See John Owen, *A Discourse Concerning Liturgies, and their Imposition* (1662) in W. H. Goold (ed.), *The Works of John Owen Vol. 15* (Edinburgh: The Banner of Truth Trust, 1965), pp. 3-57.

minister's use of his God-given gifts of extemporary prayer and exhortation.[37]   A new liturgy composed merely of 'Scripture words' was suggested, or at least an agreed revision of the old *BCP* with some variety and choice added (for which there was already some precedent in the existing Prayer Book).   As to ceremonies, they presented the standard century-old puritan objections to kneeling at the Lord's Supper, the imposition of holy days, the use of the surplice, the signing of the cross in baptism, and bowing to altars and at the name of Jesus.[38]

The Bishops answered with equal forthrightness. They contested the historical claims concerning primitive episcopacy 'balanced and managed by *authoritative* commixtion of Presbyters'[39] though they acknowledged the usefulness of some 'Assistance and Counsel of Presbyters in subordination to the Bishops.' Playing on fears of a return to civil strife, they questioned whether there really were inherent problems in the rule of one individual in the *state* as well as the church, thus casting doubt on the presbyterians' commitment to the king and strongly implying that if they had their way it would 'breed and foment perpetual Factions both in Church and State.'

As to the liturgy, they teased the presbyterians that their extemporary prayers were sometimes longer than a whole church service, and that by contending against short

---

[37] *Reliquiae Baxterianae*, Part II, pp. 234-5. This last point goes some way to answering Owen's objections in Owen, *ibid.*, pp. 10-12 that ministers gifted by Christ to his church (Ephesians 4:11) are in no need of 'stinted form of prayers' set down by man's authority to make them competent for the task.

[38] *Reliquiae Baxterianae*, Part II, p. 236.

[39] My italics. The point at issue is whether presbyters would have authority in various issues or just be permitted to give advice.

responsive prayers they were not sufficiently cognizant of 'the Infirmities of the meaner sort of People (which are the major part of most Congregations)'. Although they refuted several points made in Baxter's paper, they declared that they were not entirely against making a revision of the Prayer Book. On the issue of ceremonies, they could not see what the fuss was about, and stated that the problem was really with the ignorance of those who objected to them, and to 'the unsubduedness of some Men's Spirits, more apt to contend than willing to submit their private Opinions, to the Publick Judgment of the Church.'[40] They did not appreciate the tenderness of puritan consciences.

Despite this, the king issued the Worcester House Declaration[41] in October, indicating his willingness to consider both a form of reduced episcopacy and Prayer Book revision. Although it referred several issues to a future national synod for debate and was not at first entirely satisfactory on church government issues,[42] it granted most of the presbyterians' points, especially regarding liberty of conscience in ceremonies. This was the high water mark for the puritan cause, 'the most generous suggestion of

---

[40] *Reliquiae Baxterianae*, Part II, p. 242-247. The documents submitted can also be found in Gould, *Documents*, pp. 12-39 and in E. Cardwell, *A History of Conferences and Other Proceedings Connected with the Revision of the* Book of Common Prayer; *from the year 1558 to the year 1690* (Oxford: OUP, 1841), pp. 277-286.
[41] *His majesty's Declaration to all his loving subjects of his kingdom of England and dominion of Wales concerning ecclesiastical affairs* printed in Gould, *Documents*, pp. 63-78 (with notes of revisions made in it by the presbyterians who were permitted to see a draft); *Reliquiae Baxterianae*, Part II, pp. 259-64; and Cardwell, *History of Conferences*, pp. 286-98.
[42] See *The Petition of the Ministers to the King upon the first draft of his Declaration* and other responses in Baxter, *Reliquiae Baxterianae*, Part II, pp. 265-285 (esp. p. 269); Gould, *Documents*, pp. 79-104 (esp. p. 87).

accommodation ever made to the Puritans.'[43]   Baxter, Reynolds, and Calamy were offered bishoprics and other leading puritans proposed for important preferment.   Yet they did not all accept,[44] fearful that the Declaration was not to be trusted or depended upon as a serious blueprint for a permanent solution.[45] As one contemporary wit put it,

> God bless our good and gracious King
> Whose promise none relyes on
> Who never said A foolish thing
> Nor every did A wise one.'[46]

Charles was playing for time and trying to keep the presbyterians sweet with gracious words until a new Parliament was elected, to whom he had said he would defer. Clarendon, his Lord Chancellor, was 'still apprehensive of Presbyterian political strength and uncertain of the popularity of Puritanism',[47] and so concessions at this stage seemed wise while the future was uncertain. The re-establishment of the Church of England proceeded apace 'under cover of this

---

[43] A. Whiteman, 'The Restoration of the Church of England' in G. F. Nuttall and O. Chadwick (eds.), *From Uniformity to Unity 1662-1962* (London: SPCK, 1962), p. 67.

[44] Reynolds became Bishop of Norwich, but Baxter declined the See of Hereford.

[45] The presbyterians failed to carry a Bill in Parliament to give the Worcester House Declaration the force of law. The king considered his word to be sufficient; but then, he was drawn to the idea of an effective royal power to alter religion by fiat, so that (at a later, more convenient time perhaps) he could 'declare' further liberty for Roman Catholics.

[46] The saying is attributable to John Wilmot, Earl of Rochester (1647-1680). See *The Oxford Book of English Verse*, p. 227.

[47] A. Whiteman, 'The Restoration of the Church of England', p. 71. Whiteman thinks that in the Declaration 'detailed care is given to changes which could only be effective as long-range reforms' and so it was perhaps a serious proposal for a settled agreement, contra Bosher's more sanguine interpretation of its political expediency (Bosher, *Restoration Settlement*, p. 149 and 188ff).

feigned conciliation',[48] with more bishops and cathedral staff being appointed and increasingly widespread use of the Prayer Book. Meanwhile, other evangelical groups such as the Independents / Congregationalists and Anabaptists were infuriated with the presbyterian leaders who had resisted moves towards a general toleration in favour of their own comprehension in a national church structure.[49] In the jockeying for position and influence in the coming new order, evangelical groups inevitably disagreed on tactics and the limits of toleration. They were thus divided and soon to be conquered.

With parliamentary elections pending, much hinged on what would happen in the early months of 1661. Yet the puritan cause was dealt a blow by again being linked in the public mind with rebellion and volatility. For some time there had been talk of instability in the army and militant sectarianism amongst ex-Roundhead troops and Cromwellian officers.[50] In January 'Fifth Monarchy Men' led by Thomas Venner started out from William Taylor's parish of St Stephen's and made their way down Bishopsgate to start 'the Barbarest Insurrection that ever happened in any Kings Government, and ... the Greatest peece of impudence and grandest plot of treachery.'[51] Venner, who had plotted an

---

[48] Bosher, *Restoration Settlement*, p. 217.

[49] See Bosher, *Restoration Settlement*, p. 190 whose sources speak of Independent 'resentment and fury' at the presbyterians. Baxter is frank in mentioning the sectarian concerns and belief that the political weight of evangelical groups as a whole would have been better employed if the presbyterians had been less forward in meeting the bishops and discussing terms on their own. See *Reliquiae Baxterianae*, Part II, pp. 379-80.

[50] See, e.g. Green, *The Re-Establishment of the Church of England*, pp. 12-13.

[51] Details, with great colour and not a little Mayoral propaganda, can be read in *The Last Farewel to the Rebellious Sect called the Fifth Monarchy-Men on Wednesday January the Ninth, Together with their Treacherous Proceedings, Attempts,*

uprising against Cromwell a few years before, was now vainly attempting to replace King Charles with King Jesus in a violent coup. This only appeared to confirm the Cavalier view that the 'Good Old Cause' was not dead but merely slumbering, so Anabaptists and Quakers were dragged from their beds at midnight and thrown into prison, despite legitimate howls of protest that they had nothing to do with the extremists.[52] It took several days to put down the uprising completely, Venner's head finally being placed in a prominent position on London Bridge. Yet the threat of terror was a convenient electioneering bonus for the reactionary Anglican cause.

In London, however, anti-episcopal sentiment was inflamed by the government's overreaction and by Sheldon's behaviour as bishop; two presbyterian and two congregationalist MPs were elected at a hustings where the crowd shouted 'No Bishops! No Lord Bishops!"[53] The government was swift to react, ordering the arrest of some anti-episcopal leaders and instructing others (such as the Earl of Warwick, the patron of Essex presbyterians) to stay away from county elections which were happening at around the same time.[54] The result of these pressures and the inevitable

---

Combats, and Skirmishes at Wood Street, Bishopsgate-Street, Leadenhall and several other places. With the total Dispersing, Defeating, and utter Ruining of that Damnable and Seditious Sect in general (London, January 1660/61) downloaded from *Early English Books Online* at http://eebo.chadwyck.com/home. The quote is from p. 8.
[52] Watts, *The Dissenters*, p. 223. The Fifth Monarchy Men believed in infant baptism for a start!
[53] According to diarist Samuel Pepys. See R. Latham, *The Shorter Pepys from The Diary of Samuel Pepys, a new and complete transcription* edited by Robert Latham and William Matthews (London: Bell and Hyman, 1985), p. 124.
[54] See R. Hutton, *The Restoration: A Political and Religious History of England and Wales 1658-1667* (Oxford: Clarendon Press, 1985), pp. 152-3.

backlash against those who had held power for so long under the Commonwealth and Protectorate was the so-called 'Cavalier Parliament' which, along with the Bishops now restored to the House of Lords, would begin not only to contravene the spirit of the Declarations of Breda and Worcester House but turn to persecute the puritans.

The king was crowned on St George's Day 1661 amid great pomp and ceremony. One of the first acts of the new parliament was to order the public burning of the Solemn League and Covenant, the agreement of 1643 between Scottish covenanters and the leaders of the English parliamentarians. This had been subscribed to by many puritans, and committed them to the abolition of prelacy (the episcopal system) and the reformation of religion along puritan lines. It was in this atmosphere of resurgent Anglicanism that a group of presbyterian and Episcopalian divines met at the Bishop of London's residence at the Savoy to discuss changes in the liturgy. This was in fulfilment of the promise in the Worcester House Declaration, and charged them to consult and agree upon changes 'needful or expedient for the giving satisfaction to tender consciences ... but avoiding, as much as may be, all unnecessary alterations'.[55]

The so-called 'Savoy Conference' was not a conferring of equals joined in a common task. The bishops claimed to desire no change in the liturgy and, led by the politically savvy Sheldon, manoevred the presbyterians into the position of humble supplicants begging for exceptions. An extensive list of such exceptions to the 1604 Book of Common Prayer was

---

[55] *The King's Warrant for the Conference at the Savoy* in Gould, *Documents*, p. 109.

presented, and there is 'an air of dismissive superiority' in the whole tone of the Bishops' answers.[56] Baxter even presented an entirely new liturgy composed explicitly out of scriptural phrases so as to satisfy biblically scrupulous fellow puritans and give them options within the proposed revised book. Yet Baxter was morose about the whole affair:

> I have reason to think that the Generality of the Bishops and Doctors present never knew what we offered them in the reformed Liturgy, nor in this Reply, nor in any of our Papers, save those few which we read openly to them. For they were put up and carried away, and I conjecture scarce any but the Writers of their Confutations would be at the Labour of reading them over ... So it seems before they knew what was in them, they resolved to reject our Papers, right or Wrong, and to deliver them up to their Contradictors.[57]

This is perhaps explained by the fact that another agenda was being prosecuted elsewhere. Convocation had been called in April and had been working on a new service for adult baptism throughout May.[58] On July 9th the Commons passed a Bill of Uniformity to restore the 1604 Prayer Book without alteration and sent it to the Lords, without so much as a nod towards the proceedings still in session at the Savoy. The battle over the precise terms of the settlement was being fought on several fronts, and only the most dedicated and engaged bishop would have had time and inclination to wade

---

[56] C. Buchanan, *The Savoy Conference Revisited: the proceedings taken from the Grand Debate of 1661 and the works of Richard Baxter* (Cambridge: Grove Books, 2002), p. 7. The exceptions and answers are helpfully set out in Gould, *Documents*, pp. 111-176.

[57] *Reliquiae Baxterianae*, Part II, p. 335.

[58] See Buchanan, *Savoy Conference Revisited*, p. 9 footnote 22. Convocation was equivalent to the Church's 'parliament'.

through all the often pernickety liturgical opinions presented to them. Besides, as Whiteman points out, 'It would be difficult to find a sadder example of misapplied zeal than Baxter's determination to strive with the Anglicans almost single-handed in these discussions. Not only were his tactics misconceived; he was also already on such uneasy terms with the Anglican leaders – particularly Morley – that his criticisms and suggestions were unlikely to get a ready welcome.'[59] The tide had now turned. Episcopalian strength had now returned so decisively that there was no longer any question of attaining a compromise favourable to the puritans; it was more a matter of what could be 'salvaged from the wreck of their hopes.'[60] Concessions to the presbyterians at the Savoy were unlikely, in any case, to be ratified by the Cavalier Parliament in anti-puritan mood.[61]

Convocation debated the Prayer Book to be annexed to a new Act of Uniformity in November and December 1661. Whiteman and others claim the Book was only 'conservatively and sparingly altered'[62] and yet over 600 changes were made with only a very few tipping the hat to puritan exceptions, and many leaning in the opposite direction.[63] The 1662 Prayer

---

[59] Whiteman, 'The Restoration of the Church of England', pp. 77-78.
[60] *ibid.*, p. 78.
[61] See E. C. Ratcliff, 'The Savoy Conference and the Revision of the Book of Common Prayer' in Nuttall and Chadwick, *From Uniformity to Unity*, p. 127.
[62] Whiteman, 'The Restoration of the Church of England', p. 80.
[63] Buchanan, *Savoy Conference Revisited*, pp. 77-78 lists 17 concessions made in response to the puritans, but most are trivial or insubstantial and not all were eventually incorporated in 1662 anyway. One change that did make it in was the addition of the 'manual acts' into the Prayer of Consecration which the puritans requested in order to make the moment of consecration more explicit and distinct (see *Reliquiae Baxterianae*, Part II, p. 325). This is a declension from the removal of such 'objective' consecration in Cranmer's liturgy. Baxter's own Savoy Liturgy expresses a markedly 'higher' eucharistic doctrine than that of the 1552 or 1559 services.

Book, unlike those of previous years, possessed the authority of a National Synod of the Church of England.[64] Yet although there were some successes (the Black Rubric against transubstantiation was reinserted and clarified), it remained unacceptable to many puritans.

Baxter complained that the new book was 'more grievous than before.'[65] He particularly disliked the rubric in the baptismal liturgy affirming that it is 'certain by God's word' that baptized infants who die before committing actual sin 'are undoubtedly saved.'[66] This was not because he had no hope of infant salvation but because anyone in the parish was granted access to baptism without serious inquiry into their faith. He is clear that 'the Scruple were the less, if it were confined to the Infants of true Believers.' Indeed, he later suggested the rubric be changed to read 'True Christian Parents have no cause to doubt of the Salvation of their Children, dedicated to God in Baptism, and dying before they commit any actual sin.'[67] The Exceptions presented at Savoy objected to the post-baptismal prayer which says, 'it hath pleased thee to regenerate this infant by thy holy Spirit' because 'we cannot in Faith say, that every Child that is baptized is regenerated by God's Holy Spirit; at least it is a disputable point, and therefore we desire it may be otherwise expressed.'[68] Baxter later thought it acceptable to say the child was 'Sacramentally Regenerated'[69] and in 1679 he wrote that although full assurance and certain belief of the undoubted salvation of all infants was impossible,

---

[64] Ratcliff, 'The Savoy Conference', p. 130.
[65] *Reliquiae Baxterianae*, Part II, p. 384.
[66] cf. Ratcliff, 'The Savoy Conference', p. 145.
[67] *Reliquiae Baxterianae*, Part II, p. 428 and Part III, p. 32.
[68] *Reliquiae Baxterianae*, Part II, p. 327.
[69] *Reliquiae Baxterianae*, Part III, p. 32.

yet because the secret things of Election belong wholly to God, and the revealed things of the outward call only unto us, we according to what is revealed to us in that outward call, may and ought to judge Charitably concerning all Infants Baptized, and hope well of their Eternal State. In the general, we have good reason to believe, that God will own and bless his own Ordinances, and grant Salvation to his people in his own ways and Institutions appointed for such an end.[70]

Regardless of disputable points such as this, the liturgy contained so many objectionable elements that the puritans could never assent to it without serious reservation. The only question which remained was how assiduously it would be enforced and what level of assent would be required to its contents. At the close of the Savoy Conference, Baxter had drafted the final report of the ministers to be sent to the king. At the close of that *Petition*, he wrote, 'we... shall wait in hope, that so great a Calamity of your People, as would follow the loss of so many able faithful Ministers as rigorous Impositions would cast out, shall never be Recorded in the History of your Reign.'[71] That hope was to be dashed.

1.5.   The Great Ejection

The Act of Uniformity passed by Parliament in May 1662 was draconian and rigorous. Baxter lamented that 'a weight more grievous than a Thousand Ceremonies was added to the old Conformity, with grievous Penalty.'[72] The form of subscription required of ministers (who must now be

---

[70] *The Nonconformist Advocate*, p. 53 (Part 2).
[71] *Reliquiae Baxterianae*, Part II, p. 368; *Petition to the King at the Close of the Conference* in Gould, *Documents*, p. 385.
[72] *Reliquiae Baxterianae*, Part II, p. 384.

episcopally ordained or re-ordained) demanded 'unfeigned assent and consent to all and everything contained and prescribed' in the *Book of Common Prayer*.[73] Furthermore, it required all ministers, lecturers, and even schoolteachers to declare 'that it is not lawful, upon any pretence whatsoever, to take arms against the king ... that I will conform to the liturgy of the church of England as it is now by law established' and to renounce the oaths of the Solemn League and Covenant 'to endeavour any change or alteration of government either in church or state; and that the same was in itself an unlawful oath.'[74] This, exclaimed Baxter, would provide Rome with a perfect excuse for calling the Protestants 'a Perjured People' whose oaths could only be trusted as far as it was politically expedient.[75] Moreover, it would force them to renounce their constant 'mending' of religion and a seeking after further godly reformation even by legitimate political means.

All this was to be enacted on St Bartholomew's Day, the significance of which was not just that it recalled the French massacre of thousands of Huguenots on the same day in 1572, but that it was the day tithes and rents were due. If ministers did not conform they would lose these payments, which were made quarterly in arrears, thus impoverishing most of them at a stroke. The Act did not pass without a fight. As Seaward points out:

> presbyterian efforts to call into question convocation's work [on the new *Book of Common Prayer*] were thwarted by a

---

[73] *An Act for the Uniformity of Public Prayers and Administration of Sacraments and other Rites and Ceremonies; and for establishing the form of making, ordaining, and consecrating Bishops, Priests, and Deacons, in the Church of England*, also known as 14 Charles II, c.4, in Gould, *Documents*, p. 389.
[74] *ibid.*, p. 392.
[75] Baxter, *Reliquiae Baxterianae*, Part II, p. 384.

mere five votes; an attempt to put back the date of the implementation of the Bill to Michaelmas (which would have allowed ejected ministers the benefit of rents which then fell due) was lost by nine votes ... the proviso for allowing fifths to expelled ministers were struck out, the latter by only seven votes. But defeat by so small a margin remained defeat.[76]

The majorities were not so large as to dissuade further attempts at leniency or toleration in future, but they were decisive for now. The anti-puritan circle in the church, in Parliament, and at court was able effectively to cajole those fearful of further uprisings or of constant instability into suppressing the presbyterians and sects. Clarendon himself declared that he was,

no Friend to Force and Violence especially in Matters of Conscience ... For what can be more pernicious to the safety of any Kingdom than to have within it self so great a body as all the dissenters in England make, continually exasperated by Penalties and invaded by a legal kind of Hostility ...? Compulsion may bring many Hypocrites, but no real Converts into our Church ... Nothing does more Efficaciously dispose and prepare the minds of Men for Treason and Rebellion, than by Force to make them Act against their Conscience in matters of Religion ... Let us not therefore give them that only advantage they have over us, which is of suffering for their Religion.[77]

---

[76] P. Seaward, *The Cavalier Parliament and the Reconstruction of the Old Regime, 1661-1667* (Cambridge: CUP, 1989), p. 178 cf. p. 193. Re: 'fifths', sequestered clergy in the 1640s were entitled to a 'pension' of a fifth of their former livings when they were ejected.

[77] Edward Hyde, Earl of Clarendon, *Second Thoughts, or the Case for a Limited*

Yet if it was the Lord Chancellor's aim to avoid a rigid, unaccommodating settlement, he had failed.[78] Of the Uniformity Bill debates in Parliament he wrote that, 'Every man according to his passion, thought of adding something to it that make it more grievous to somebody whom he did not love.'[79] A. G. Matthews, the soundest authority on the numbers, determined that at least 936 ministers were thus deprived of their livings in 1662. With a further 129 deprived at an uncertain date (between 1660-1663) and with the ejections of 1660 as well, a total of 1760 ministers (about 20% of the whole) were thrust out of the Church of England, silenced from preaching or teaching by law and thus deprived of livelihood.[80] As Gerald Bray comments, 'Almost all of these were Puritans, and so the Act may be said to represent the expulsion of Puritanism from the national Church.'[81] A momentous and sad day indeed.

Why did almost all the puritans go? We may get a glimpse of their reasoning by opening up a letter from one 'A. B.', a minister who in 1662 wrote to a 'lady of quality' to justify his reasons for Non-conformity.[82] A. B. was not the

---

Toleration stated according to the present Exigence in Affairs of Church and State (1660) downloaded from *Early English Books Online* at http://eebo.chadwyck.com/home. The quote is from pp. 3 and 10. I am not convinced that EEBO has correctly identified the date of this document, as it seems to me to fit a slightly later date.

[78] See Whiteman, 'The Restoration of the Church of England', p. 81; Bosher, *Restoration Settlement*, p. 253ff; Seaward, *Cavalier Parliament*, pp. 163-195.

[79] H. Craik, *The Life of Edward Earl of Clarendon, Lord High Chancellor of England volume 2* (BiblioBazaar, 2006), p. 119.

[80] Matthews, *Calamy Revised*, pp. xii-xiii. Baxter's estimate was that 1800-2000 ministers were 'Silenced and Cast out.'

[81] Bray, *Documents*, p. 547.

[82] A. B., *A Letter from a Minister to a Person of Quality, shewing some Reasons for his Non-conformity* downloaded from *Early English Books Online* at http://eebo.chadwyck.com/home. The letter begins 'Madam', thus indicating a

Revd. Arthur Barham, Vicar of St Helen's, Bishopsgate who (as we saw earlier) had already faced some pressure from the Bishop of London, but turns out to be Richard Baxter;[83] yet certainly his objections are generically puritan ones shared by many of the ejected ministers.

He gives three reasons for his non-conformity: the *Book of Common Prayer*, the oath against rebellion, and the oath against the Solemn League and Covenant. His letter focuses only on objections to the *Book of Common Prayer*, and enumerates several reasons why he cannot subscribe to it. For starters, he cannot give 'unfeigned consent and assent to all and every thing' in it for 'here is as much fully to be declared concerning the Book of Common-Prayer, as possibly can be concerning the Book of God, the Bible itself.' It is presumptuous of 'mortal erring men, like unto our selves', Protestants even, who protest against the Pope's infallibility, to 'assume unto themselves an infallible spirit' and require such a Declaration. Had such persuasion of the set liturgy's

---

female recipient.

[83] 'A. B.' was a literary convention meaning something like 'Anonymous'. It was peculiarly appropriate here, since the Act of Uniformity required subscription to made thus: 'I, **A.B.**, do here declare...' where A.B. means 'insert name here' (see the Act in Gould, *Documents*, pp. 389 and 392 for instance and the page of similar oaths in Baxter, *Reliquiae Baxterianae*, Part II, p. 395). In 1679 Baxter wrote a work called *The Nonconformist's Plea for Peace or An Account of their judgment in certain things in which they are misunderstood...*and he mentions that he wrote other such works and published letters on the subject in *Reliquiae Baxterianae*, Part III, pp. 187-188. One of these is called *The Nonconformists Advocate: Or, A Farther Account of their Judgment in Certain things in which they are misunderstood.* **Written Principally in Vindication of *A LETTER* from a Minister to a Person of Quality, shewing some Reasons for his Nonconformity** which defends the author's original letter. It does not name Baxter on the title page, although it bears all the marks of being his and is ascribed to him by EEBO on the basis of Halkett and Laing's identification in S. Halkett and J. Laing, *Dictionary of Anonymous and Pseudonymous Literature of Great Britain* (4 vols, Edinburgh, 1882-1888), second edition, errata p. [4].

perfection been required of previous generations they too would not have conformed or submitted to it, 'conscience being now much more forced and violated'. 'Though for peace sake I could swallow down some gnats, and make no bones of them', he says, yet he cannot be forced to say they are not in actual fact gnats or avouch that he loves to swallow them!

A. B. continues, explaining that he has no objections to a set liturgy as such, but only to the terms of 'assent and consent' required to be given to this one; for that would be to declare 'the truth and rightfulness of it... the goodness, the expediency and behoofulness of it' without being able to disagree in even the slightest detail – 'no, not so much as in pointing the Psalms'. He would rather 'eat hot fire coals' than do that because several things in the book are not right, true, good, or expedient.[84] The things he then scruples are:

> 1. The use of the Apocrypha – that it is to be read so much and all under the name of holy Scripture, while 'some Books of the Sacred Canon are wholly left out and never to be read' publicly in church. The legendary book 'Bel and the Dragon' had been re-inserted into the Calendar of readings in 1662, for instance, despite the use of the Apocrypha being one of the puritans' biggest bug-bears.[85]

---

[84] Seaward, *Cavalier Parliament*, p. 189 notes 'Nonconformists had vigorously objected to the assent and consent clause: they were prepared to read the Common Prayer as they were obliged, but reluctant by declaring their assent and consent to imply that they believed it perfect.'

[85] Before the war, a Committee of the House of Lords (of which Calamy had been a member according to Buchanan, *Savoy Conference Revisited*, p. 5) had drawn up a list of doctrinal and practical issues to be addressed in the Prayer Book, one of which was 'whether lessons of canonical Scripture should be put into the Kalendar

2.   His next objections relate to the Baptism liturgy: that it strictly requires godparents (where Scripture does not) and hardly mentions fathers (which Scripture explicitly does); that the signing of the cross gives the impression that 'baptizing with water were not sufficient of itself' which is 'preposterous and very dangerous... too like a Sacrament upon a Sacrament' when Protestants should distinguish themselves from 'the Idolatrous Papists; who superstitiously adore the Cross, foolishly, fondly, and wickedly signing themselves with it upon every occasion, thinking themselves no good Catholicks without so doing'; and that concerning the rubric which declares baptized infants who die before committing actual sin are saved 'I know no such word in Scripture; no such word as will give me a certainty of persuasion beyond all possibility of doubting.' He goes to some lengths to lampoon this idea, as if such a doctrine gave mothers an excuse to kill their babies and thereby secure their eternal life, or ministers an excuse to baptise even Turks or Jews regardless of true faith.[86]

3.   The order for the burial of the dead is objectionable because of its too great a charitable presumption to be extended to everyone buried using this rite. 'Scripture saith expressly, That neither Adulterers, nor Fornicators, nor Drunkards, shall ever go to Heaven; yet in a perfect opposition, when I bury a known Adulterer, Fornicator, Drunkard, I must declare and

---

instead of Apocrypha'. See Cardwell, *History of Conferences*, p. 274. Cardwell p. 380 and Gould, *Documents*, p. 456 note the insertion of Bel and the Dragon in the 1662 Table of Lessons.

[86] We noted above that Baxter was against this rubric, and his careful reasoning.

avouch that *his soul is assuredly gone thither*. I dare not thus damn a person while he is living, and yet save him when he is dead... Alas, I am so far from having *any sure and certain hope of his Resurrection unto eternal life and salvation*, that I rather *have a sure and certain fear of his Resurrection unto eternal death and damnation.*'

Buchanan avers that '[t]he requirements of renunciation of the Solemn League and Covenant and of undergoing Episcopal ordination were in all probability the major factors' leading to the exodus of puritans from the Church of England.[87] Those assuredly were important issues. Yet A. B.'s letter, at least, does not even get around to those factors; after a brief mention of the Covenant at the start, all four large pages are devoted to issues of liturgy and doctrine.[88]

A. B. was not Arthur Barham, but it was indeed for these same sorts of reasons that St Helen's was deprived of its senior minister. Barham had once considered a career in the law, but when his father died he sold his law books and went to Cambridge where 'he studied divinity with great diligence and delight.' He was presented to St Helen's by Sir John Langham, to whom he was related by marriage, in 1647 and was minister there for fifteen years, 'preaching with great success.'[89] He was a Presbyterian, and had participated in the proceedings of the London Provincial Assembly 'actively and

---

[87] Buchanan, *Savoy Conference Revisited*, p. 10. William Taylor of Coleman Street, for instance, resisted Sheldon's pressure to be episcopally ordained. See Seaward, 'Gilbert Sheldon and the London Vestries', p. 62.

[88] In Baxter's 'Epistle to the Reader' in *The Nonconformists Advocate* he explains that he only had a few days to research and write his response to the 'lady of quality', which may explain this.

[89] See Palmer, *The Nonconformist's Memorial: volume 1*, p. 114. Cf. *Annals of St Helen's*, p. 315.

consistently,'[90] but now his energy would have to be directed outside the established church. The Act of Uniformity also denied the academy and the church the talents of men like John Owen, Richard Baxter, John Bunyan, Thomas Watson, and Stephen Charnock. 'We should greatly underestimate the seriousness of 1662' writes Iain Murray, 'if we imagined that the cleavage which then took place was only over phrases in the Book of Common Prayer and forms of Church order. These things were involved, but the Puritans regarded them as only a part of a much wider issue, namely, what is the nature of true Christianity? The Nonconformists believed that in acting as they did they were acting for the Gospel.'[91]

The theme of loss comes into the farewell sermons of the ejected; not just the relational loss that a pastor feels when torn away from his people, but the loss of the gospel which results when pulpits go silent. So the sermon for which Edmund Calamy was thrown in prison asks:

> Wherein does England excel other places? There is more wealth in Turkey than in England, and the heathen nations have more of the glory of the world than any Christian king has. What is the glory of England? Is it not Christianity? What is the glory of Christianity but the gospel? If the

---

[90] T. Liu *Puritan London: A Study of Religion and Society in the City Parishes* (London: Associated University Presses, 1986), p. 84. The Provincial Assembly was roughly the equivalent of the current (Anglican) London Diocesan Synod, only one step removed from the National Assembly (never constituted in England) in a Presbyterian system of church government. Liu comments that the Presbyterian system did not establish itself very effectively in the City since the laity at St Helen's and St Andrew's did not join in the Presbyterian system with enthusiasm. These were 'among the substantial parochial communities' at the time but produced no 'staunch Presbyterian civic leaders'.
[91] I. Murray, *Sermons of the Great Ejection* (Edinburgh: Banner of Truth, 1962), pp. 7-8.

gospel be gone, our glory is gone.[92]

After spending several minutes outlining the effects of the potential loss of the gospel (in phrases strikingly similar to Calamy's at times), Thomas Brooks asked his congregation whether God was removing the gospel from England by this dreadful ejection. 'It is the fear of many; but I humbly suppose he will not' he affirmed. Of the nine reasons he then gives for this confidence, the third is:

> The ineffectiveness of all former attempts and designs to destroy the gospel. You know what endeavours of old there has been to darken the sun, to put out the light of heaven, in the Marian days, and in other days since then; and yet it has defied prisons, racks, flames, pillories, or anything else to extinguish the glory of it.[93]

To this, in his last sermon at St Stephen's, Walbrook, Thomas Watson adds:

> What are all the sufferings we can undergo in the world in comparison with eternity?[94]

And so it was with truly 'evangelical' sentiments such as these that Samuel Lee and Peter Sterry, both sometime lecturers at St Helen's, Bishopsgate were forced to give up preaching.[95] Lee, a former Oxford don and 'master of physic and alchymy' as well as a theologian of some note, was licensed in 1666 'to go to America, the Caribbee islands, and 'other western parts for the improvement of his knowledge by his search and collection of the rarities as well of art as nature in the remoter parts of the other world" and continued to

---

[92] *ibid.*, p. 30.
[93] *ibid.*, p. 42.
[94] *ibid.*, p. 146.
[95] *Calamy Revised*, pp. 321 and 463 respectively.

write books of both a pastoral and learned nature.[96] William Blackmore, the Rector of St Peter's, Cornhill also had to leave, after 16 years in that parish. He was not an especially gripping preacher, his parishioners once complaining that 'we cannot nor ought to be so unfaithful to our soules as to starve and pine them under soe dull and heavie a ministry'; yet he was 'a considerable man' among London Presbyterians and remained in the City, settling in the parish of St Botolph's, Aldersgate.[97]

Richard Kidder was deprived for nonconformity, but in his *Autobiography* states that he did not receive a copy of the new Prayer Book until September 1662 though 'intirely satisfied in Episcopacy, and with a liturgy.'[98] This was a problem in many places since, as Calamy writes,

> the Common Prayer book with the alterations and amendments … did not come out of the press till a few days before the 24th August. So that of the seven thousand ministers in England who kept their livings, few, except those who were in or near London could possibly have a sight of the book with its alterations, till after they had declared their assent and consent to it.[99]

Provision was later made for men like Kidder, who afterwards was able to conform and serve as Rector of St Martin, Outwich,[100] eventually becoming Bishop of Bath and Wells in

---

[96] *ibid.*, p. 321. For his impressive mastery of biblical languages and Latin, and reference to his expertise in 'physic and alchymy' see S. Palmer, *The Nonconformist's Memorial: Volume 1* (London: W. Harris, 1775), pp. 95-96.
[97] *Calamy Revised*, p. 59.
[98] *ibid.*, p. 307.
[99] Quoted in Gould, *Documents*, p. 459. See also Green, *The Re-Establishment of the Church of England*, pp. 145-147. 24th August is St Bartholomew's Day, when the Act came into force.
[100] *Calamy Revised*, p. 379. Reference to his time at St Martin, Outwich only

1691. The king attempted to mitigate the force of the Act even in 1662, claiming that in order to fulfil his previous promise of liberty to tender consciences he would use 'that power of dispensing, which we conceive to be inherent in us.'[101] Parliament, however, even a Cavalier one, baulked at this potentially troublesome precedent of allowing the king to arbitrarily apply widespread exemptions to their legislation, and nullified his declaration; yet the issue of the monarch's power to grant indulgence would return in future years. For now, the die was cast and there was no going back. It remained to be seen whether alienating and impoverishing[102] so many in the dissenting community would result in a renewal of the kind of social, political, and religious unrest which had sent Charles on his travels during the Civil War.[103]

2. Part Two: The Great Persecution

2.1. The Clarendon Code

The government continued attempts to moderate the surprising harshness of the Act of Uniformity until 1663.

---

comes in the entry for Thomas Pakeman.

[101] *The King's Declaration* in Gould, *Documents*, p. 464.

[102] As previously mentioned, ministers were denied their payments due on St Bartholomew's Day and so were left without means. Not all suffered penury. One ejected minister, 'A Man of great Courage and Boldness' called Thomas Andrews not only had to deal with Quaker hecklers and an assassination attempt but combined his pastoral gifts with financial acumen, as Calamy writes: 'His Frugality while he continu'd the Incumbent, sav'd him some hundreds of Pounds against his Ejectment: so that he was better provided for than many of his Brethren...' *Calamy Revised*, p. 11.

[103] New regiments were recruited to the Army during the autumn just in case. See Seaward, *Cavalier Parliament*, p. 180.

Then a group of frustrated dissenters in the north plotted to overthrow Clarendon and the bishops and restore religious toleration. An informer claimed there was a plot to murder bishops and deans and clergymen; a conspiracy to seize York Castle was thwarted by the arrest of the ringleaders; and finally in October 1663 a planned nationwide rising 'dwindled to a pathetic gathering of some 200 men at Farnley Wood near Leeds.'[104] Such abortive coups were not the start of a new civil war. Some regarded them as merely comical, although the government could not afford to laugh since this was the largest and most serious rebellion since the Restoration.[105] In January 1664 over twenty conspirators were executed, but as well as untamed radicals itching for a fight the conspiracies also included a good number of presbyterians. 'The government quickly withdrew from any plans for moderating the religious laws,' says Seaward, and from 1664 onwards 'Clarendon seems to have closed his doors to the presbyterian and independent leaders whom he had welcomed before.'[106]

This was the impetus behind what became known in the nineteenth century as the Clarendon Code, a repressive series of measures against nonconformists passed during Clarendon's tenure as Lord Chancellor. The nomenclature may be unfair to Clarendon who did not necessarily initiate the cruel and oppressive legislation,[107] but he allowed the persecutors in Parliament and the Church to have their way,

---

[104] Watts, *The Dissenters*, p. 225.
[105] Seaward, *Cavalier Parliament*, p. 190. Watts calls this the Derwentdale Plot after the place it seemingly first began (in Durham). Seaward calls it the Yorkshire Plot, since it ended near Leeds (Yorkshire).
[106] Seaward, *ibid.*, p. 190.
[107] J. Coffey, *Persecution and Toleration in Protestant England, 1558-1689* (London: Longman, 2000), pp. 167-168.

on his watch, in order to prevent the law falling into disrepute through lack of effective implementation. Thus did the reign of the first English king to preach the virtues of religious toleration come to be marked by 'the calculated and often malicious persecution of Dissent.'[108] The Corporation Act of 1661 had already begun to fence off the establishment from dissenters: it aimed at restricting public offices to members of the Church of England, ensuring that no-one could be legally elected to government or municipal office without taking the Lord's Supper at least once a year according to the rites of the Church of England, subscribing the oaths of allegiance and supremacy, swearing belief in the doctrine of passive obedience (against rebellion), and renouncing the Solemn League and Covenant. Clearly aimed at presbyterians, this Act also effectively disenfranchised other consientious dissenters and Roman Catholics.

In May 1664, the Derwentdale-Yorkshire Plots were used to justify the passing of an act against 'conventicles', religious meetings for prayer, preaching, and Bible study held in meeting houses, homes, or even fields outside the auspices of the Church of England.[109] A similar act *to retaine the Queenes Majestyes Subjects in their due Obedience* of 1593 had been used against dissenters in 1660 and John Bunyan was to remain in prison until 1672 under this provision. The new Act went further in proscribing such meetings. A family could have Bible study and prayer together, along with their household servants, and be joined by up to four visitors. If

---

[108] Watts, *The Dissenters*, p. 222.
[109] The Act explicitly says it is aimed against 'disloyall persons who under pretence of Tender Consciences doe at their Meetings contrive Insurrections as late experience hath shewed.' *An Act to prevent and suppresse seditious Conventicles*, Statutes of the Realm: volume 5: 1628-80 (1819), pp. 516-20.

the number hearing a Bible reading and joining in prayer should exceed that, and they were caught, large fines could be imposed, and even imprisonment. For a third offence they could even be 'transported beyond the Seas to any of His Majestyes Forreigne Plantations' for up to seven years.[110]

Some dissenters gave up meeting illegally and contented themselves with attendance at the parish church. Others carried on meeting as they pleased. Still others attended both the parish church and conventicles, employing various tactics to guard against being caught. For instance, Adam Martindale, known for his mathematical skill, 'divided his auditors into small groups and preached the same sermon four or five times a day.'[111] Obadiah Grew dictated a new sermon to a secretary every week and 'sent it to be read, to four or more Writers in short Hand, every Saturday Night, or Lord's Day Morning; and every one of these read it to four new Men who transcrib'd it also: And so it was afterwards read at twenty several Meetings.'[112] Some met at 2 o'clock in the morning; the Congregational Church in Stepney had a concealed room in the ceiling of a meeting place; and the Dissenters at Olney met at 'three counties point' where Buckinghamshire, Bedfordshire, and Northamptonshire converge so as to be able to escape from one to the other quickly should the police arrive from one of the counties!

The Broadmead Baptists in Bristol were constantly harassed by the mayor, but eluded his violent attempts at break-ins with stealthy escapes through cellars and cupboards

---

[110] *ibid.*

[111] Watts, *The Dissenters*, p. 229. His mathematical talent is praised in *Calamy Revised*, p. 343.

[112] *Calamy Revised*, p. 236.

into hidden rooms.[113] After losing several pastors to prison for preaching at conventicles, and not wishing to close their meetings to outsiders and so lose great opportunities for the gospel 'we contrived,' they write, 'a curtain, to be hung in the meeting place ... if any informer was privately in the room as a hearer, he might hear him that spake, but could not see him, and thereby not know him.'[114] More ingeniously, 'Brother Gifford's people took this course: a company of tall brethren stand about him that speaks, and having near his feet made a trap-door in the floor, when the informers come they let down the brother that spake into a room below.'[115] It could be an exciting, if terrifying, church life and naturally not all were happy to endure such persecution. The *Broadmead Records* report that in 1665 six of their members were to be excommunicated from the church, 'some for neglecting their duty of assembling through fear'.[116]

Such fear seemed reasonable when, as Watts says, '[t]he penal code was often enforced with quite unnecessary malice and brutality.'[117] When the plague struck London in 1665, many clergy quite understandably left the city. Many nonconformist ministers remained behind and stepped into their vacated pulpits or set up their own to give spiritual solace to dying, bereaved, and frightened people. One of these brave souls was Samuel Annesley, ejected from St Giles Cripplegate in 1662. He is said later to have had a meeting place in St Helen's Place and perhaps preached there at this

---

[113] E. B. Underhill, *The Records of a Church of Christ Meeting in Broadmead, Bristol 1640-1687* (London: J. Haddon, 1847), p. 77.
[114] *ibid.*, p. 226. This is reported in the section of the book on 1674-5 after the Second Conventicles Act.
[115] *ibid.*, p. 227.
[116] *Ibid.*, p. 86.
[117] Watts, *The Dissenters*, p. 232.

time.[118] Men like him and Thomas Watson, and even congregationalists like John Owen and Thomas Goodwin who had previously kept a low profile, convened meetings to preach to people in this hour of need. Parliament, sitting at a safe distance in Oxford, was outraged at such impudence; the notorious Five Mile Act was passed, banishing all dissenting ministers from an area of five miles around any towns and corporations with which they had had previous ministerial connections. This made life very difficult, especially for those who had preached in several churches in a neighbourhood. Arthur Barham felt compelled to leave his wife and children in Hackney and move to his family home in Sussex. Thomas Watson, on the other hand, took the way out offered by the government: along with a few dozen others, he swore the 'Oxford Oath'[119] renouncing even peaceful political protest against the way the church or state was governed in return for permission to live in London.

Enforcement of the penal laws against dissenters was never as rigid as it might have been, and varied from place to place and from time to time depending on the attitude of

---

[118] See *Reliquiae Baxterianae*, Part III, p. 19 and *Calamy Revised*, pp. 13-14. Married with 24 children (only three of which survived him), his younger daughter was called Susanna, and is famous as the mother of John and Charles Wesley. Another of his daughters married the notorious Dangerfield, unbeknown to her father. According to Baxter, Annesley 'is a most sincere, godly, humble Man, totally devoted to God' (*Reliquiae Baxterianae*, Part III, p. 95).

[119] The oath reads as follows: 'I A B doe sweare That it is not lawfull upon any pretence whatsoever to take Armes against the King And that I doe abhorr that Traiterous Position of takeing Armes by His Authoritie against His Person or against those that are coo[m]missionated by Him in pursuance of such Coo[m]missions And that I will not at any time endeavour any Alteration of Goverment either in Church or State.' *An Act for restraining Non-Conformists from inhabiting in Corporations*, Statutes of the Realm: volume 5: 1628-80 (1819), p. 575. See Baxter's comments on the Oath, which is very similar to the *Et Cetera* Oath of 1640, in *Reliquiae Baxterianae*, Part III, pp. 4ff.

local officials.[120]   Even so, more than 200 of the ejected ministers ended up in jail, along with countless lay people.[121] In a letter to William Popple, poet Andrew Marvell famously described the Second (more rigidly enforced) Conventicles Act as 'the Quintessence of arbitrary Malice.' What was clear is that

> Anglican persecutors could now appeal to "a formidable legal arsenal which, potentially, made possible a Puritan holocaust." Although the worst possibilities were never realised, the Restoration did witness a persecution of Protestants by protestants without parallel in seventeenth-century Europe. [122]

It is a wonder that more did not emigrate to America, as many had done in the 1630s. Thomas Gilbert (chaplain of Magdalen College, Oxford 1650-60) was offered a position in New England. Yet, he said, 'were I worthy that dignity I think I ought rather at present to frame myselfe to suffer in Old, than to reign in New England.'[123]   As Coffey points out, 'Dissenters generally chose to stay put and face up to persecution. The longing for a theocracy had been displaced

---

[120] See *The Autobiography of Richard Baxter* (Keeble edition) p. 222, as well as Coffey, *Persecution and Toleration*, p. 170.

[121] Coffey, *Persecution and Toleration*, p. 170. Jail was not always as bad as it might have been. Although many did die in prison, Baxter's time in jail in 1670 was not so unhappy and, he says, 'my Wife was never so cheerful a Companion to me as in Prison, and *was very much against my seeking to be released...*' *Reliquiae Baxterianae*, Part III, p. 50 (my italics). Coffey quotes Terry Waite comparing his own confinement to Bunyan's with these words: 'My word, Bunyan, you're a lucky fellow'! (p. 175).

[122] Coffey, *Persecution and Toleration*, p. 169 quoting M. Goldie, 'The search for religious liberty, 1640-1690', in J. Morrill, ed., *The Oxford Illustrated History of Tudor and Stuart Britain* (Oxford, 1996), p. 300.

[123] *Calamy Revised*, p. 221.

by a sense that tribulation was the lot of the godly.'[124]

The plague of 1665 was followed in 1666 by the Great Fire of London, as 'the best, and one of the fairest Cities in the world was turn'd into Ashes and Ruines in Three Days space.'[125] The year had already been forecast to be one of destiny, as Calamy alluded to in his farewell sermon[126] and the 'blazing stars' (comets) which appeared in 1664 and 1665 are often linked in the narrative to the devastations and persecutions of these years.[127] Baxter recounted these tragic events and lamented, 'Yet, under all these desolations, the wicked are hardened', calling upon London and other cities to review the Corporation Act 'AND SPEEDILY REPENT'.[128] Charles II's own well-publicised immorality was also blamed for these and other disasters, such as the shocking defeat in the Second Anglo-Dutch War (1665-67). Clarendon himself was the scapegoat in 1667. In 1668, 'the Bawdy House Riots saw London crowds attacking brothels in order to protest against a government which had tolerated prostitution whilst persecuting devout believers.'[129] England seemed to be straining under the weight of internal, external, and divine

---

[124] Coffey, *Persecution and Toleration*, p. 177. He claims that only fifteen ministers crossed the Atlantic and just ten settled in the Netherlands. See Matthews, *Calamy Revised*, p. xiv.

[125] Baxter, *Reliquiae Baxterianae*, Part III, p. 16.

[126] See Murray, *Sermons*, p. 33: 'there are great thoughts of heart as to when God will deliver His people, and set His churches at liberty; and many men talk much of the year 1666. Some say that shall be the year in which Antichrist shall be destroyed. And there are strange impressions upon the hearts of many learned men as to that year.'

[127] See Underhill, *Broadmead Records*, p. 84 and the diagram of the orientation of the comets there. Baxter also mentions the stars in *Reliquiae Baxterianae*, Part II, p. 448 and adds to the list of terrible portents 'the driest Winter, Spring and Summer that ever Man alive knew.'

[128] *Reliquiae Baxterianae*, Part II, p. 448 (emphasis original).

[129] Coffey, *Persecution and Toleration*, p. 171.

pressure. Something would soon have to give.

2.2. *The Respite of 1672*

After a decade of persecution, there was a loosening of the strain, albeit a brief one, in 1672. Charles published a Declaration of Indulgence, stating that:

> it being evident by the sad experience of twelve years, that there is little fruit of all those forcible courses [undertaken to reduce 'all erring or dissenting persons'], we think ourself obliged to make use of that supreme power in ecclesiastical matters, which is not only inherent in us, but hath been declared and recognised to be so.[130]

Cardwell comments that this declaration 'is an instance, among many, of the dishonest and tortuous policy by which the king endeavoured to accomplish his purposes. It seems to have been intended for the benefit of the non-conformists; but was really designed to relieve the Romanists.'[131] Though Charles may have felt some sympathy for the sufferings of the dissenters, he had in actual fact bound himself by secret clauses in a treaty with Louis XIV of France in 1670. These clauses gave him financial and military backing from the French to facilitate a re-Catholicisation of England in return for his own promises to convert to Roman Catholicism, ease the burden on English Catholics, and to aid the French in what became the Third Anglo-Dutch War. This was, needless to say, a secret at the time for if the Protestant dissenters had known of such

---

[130] E. Cardwell, *Documentary Annals of the Reformed Church of England being a collection of injunctions, declarations, orders, articles of inquiry, &c. from the year 1546 to 1716; with notes historical and explanatory* (Oxford: OUP, 1839), p. 283.
[131] *ibid.*, p. 282.

purposes they would clearly have resisted them.[132]   The Indulgence was designed to loosen the penal laws against the Roman Catholics and to deflect attention from this (and even create sympathy for it) by granting greater indulgence to the dissenters.

There was some hesitation on the nonconformists' side. They were offered, by this Royal Proclamation, a form of official toleration, an opportunity to have legally licensed ministers and meeting-houses, and a suspension of the penal laws against them. Around 500 Dissenters were pardoned, including John Bunyan who was finally released from his twelve year stretch in prison.[133]   Some were concerned, however, not just that the method of granting them this liberty savoured too much of arbitrary dictatorship, but also that the information about their meetings and ministers thus provided to the government might be used against them in future, and not without warrant.[134]   Yet eventually the offer was taken up and a total of 1610 ministers took out licences, including 939 Presbyterians, 458 Congregationalists or

---

[132] The terms of the secret treaty were revealed in 1682. See G. Clarke, *The Later Stuarts 1660-1714* (Oxford: OUP, 1956), p. 79. Clarke comments that Englishmen who disagreed about lots of things were united in fearing three enemies which they believed to be closely allied: popery, France, and arbitrary power.

[133] According to Robert Oliver, 'Another two years of imprisonment followed from 1674 to 1676 before Bunyan was finally released largely as a result of John Owen's intercession with the Bishop of Lincoln.' See R. Oliver, "Grace Abounding' – Imputed Righteousness in the Life and Work of John Bunyan' in *Churchman 107/1* (1993), p. 72.

[134] See the letter of Gilbert Sheldon, now Archbishop of Canterbury, to Bishop Henchman of London in 1676 concerning the number of dissenters where he requires the information so that, 'the just number of dissenters being known, their suppression will be a work very practicable' in Cardwell, *Documentary Annals*, p. 291. See also the comments in K. W. H. Howard (ed.), *The Axminster Ecclesiastica 1660-1698* (Sheffield: Gospel Tidings Publications, 1976 [1874]), p. 28 about Sheldon's attempt to keep an eye on the ejected of 1660-1662.

Independents, and 210 Baptists.[135]

Arthur Barham returned to his family in Hackney and was licensed to preach at his house there. *The Annals of St Helen's* record that he 'preached in his own house twice every Lord's Day, catechized in the afternoon, and expounded some portion of Scripture in the evening. Besides which he preached a Lecture every Friday, catechized two days in the week, and performed family duty every morning in two, and sometimes in three, families besides his own.'[136] The pastor of Broadmead Baptist Church worked equally hard, preaching four or five times a week.[137] Barham was joined in Hackney by other ejected ministers newly licensed there: Jonathan Tuckney whose father was buried in St Andrew's, Undershaft;[138] Peter Sterry, former Chaplain to Oliver Cromwell and Lecturer at St Helen's, who was not, however, to live beyond November; Samuel Lee, another former Lecturer at St Helen's was licensed nearby in Newington Green;[139] and Thomas Woodcock, the ejected Rector of St Andrew, Undershaft, lived in Hackney but is not recorded as having been licensed in 1672.[140]

Meanwhile, dissenting meeting-houses were built and fitted out for public use. Thomas Watson had been able to

---

[135] Figures from Coffey, *Persecution and Toleration*, p. 172. A few, like Baxter, accepted a licence but refused to accept a label.

[136] Cox, *Annals of St Helen's*, p. 315.

[137] *Broadmead Records*, p. 94.

[138] *Calamy Revised*, p. 496 records that Jonathan was 'a Man of Good Learning, yet he was render'd useless by Melancholy.'

[139] He later became the pastor of a church in Rhode Island for 4 years, but when sailing from Boston in October 1691 he was captured by French privateers and died at St Malo. *Calamy Revised*, p. 321.

[140] He is, however, recorded as being fined for preaching 'at the meeting-house, Hackney' in 1682. *Calamy Revised*, p. 543.

build such a meeting house (in the wake of the Great Fire) at Devonshire House, Bishopsgate. This was popular enough to require two galleries, but was maliciously seized for episcopalian use in 1671. So Watson was licensed at his house in Dowgate in 1672.[141] He was also joined by another famous puritan author, Stephen Charnock (former fellow of New College, Oxford) in pastoring a Presbyterian congregation at Crosby Hall, Bishopsgate literally a few paces away from St Helen's.[142] The Hall belonged to Alderman Sir John Langham now patron to the nonconformists who 'retained it as a place of worship upwards of a century ... Doctor Grosvenor, another pastor, had a congregation so numerous and opulent, that the annual collection used to exceed that of any Presbyterian Church in London.'[143] Another such nonconformist church was located just a stone's throw away in St Helen's Place, the licensed ministers there being Samuel Annesley (Wesley's grandfather) whose son Peter preached at St Helen's in 1676, and later John Woodhouse.[144]

St Helen's itself was now in the possession of Thomas Horton, who had been ejected as head of Queens' College, Cambridge in 1660 and silenced in 1662. He afterwards conformed, and in 1666 had filled the nearly three year interregnum at St Helen's following the resignation of

---

[141] *Calamy Revised*, p. 513.

[142] *Calamy Revised*, pp. 111-112. The location of the Hall (or Chapel), Crosby Square, survives as a tiny road off Great St Helen's.

[143] Cox, *Annals of St Helen's*, p. 333. Dr Grosvenor was at Crosby Hall in 1704-49 according to p. 338. The *Annals* refer to a congregation there, gathered by Watson, from as early as 'soon after the Act of Uniformity'.

[144] Woodhouse, says *Calamy Revised*, succeeded Annesley as minister at 'Little St Helen's', whereas p. 13 gives Annesley's meeting place as at 'what is now St Helen's Place'.

Barham's successor in October 1663.[145] He had been 'a noted Tutor to young Presbyterian scholars' at Emmanuel College, Cambridge, 'a pious and learned man, a hard student, and a sound divine, well accomplished for the work of the ministry, and very conscientious in the discharge of it.' According to a manuscript relating to the ecclesiastical parties of the day, 'Doctor Horton is Minister of St Helen's, he hath a very great congregation of half-conformists, in whom he hath much interest. He is a man of very good learning, and a constant, laborious preacher.'[146] After him, Richard Kidder sometimes officiated at St Helen's in the 1670s and,

> found many of his communicants 'kneeled not at the sacrament, but were otherwise very devout and regular'. The practice had been indulged by their previous minister, Dr Horton. The communions were 'very great ... and great summs of money given to the poor at those times,' and considering 'the mischief of dismissing such a number of Communicants and sending them to the Non-Conformists', Kidder decided to continue to give the sacrament to those who refused to kneel, and risk being suspended for it.[147]

It was such local variations in practice due to conscientious puritan objections that led to the call, from moderate Anglicans like Kidder, for indulgence. Parliament, while not insensible to the pleas for toleration from the

---

[145] John Sybbald. I have yet to discover the reason he resigned.

[146] On Horton see Cox, *Annals of St Helen's*, p. 316. He does not appear in *Calamy Revised* despite what is said in the *Annals* about his 'silencing'. It is interesting to note that St Helen's today might also be characterised by some as a large congregation of half-conformists!

[147] T. Harris, *London Crowds in the Reign of Charles II: Propaganda and Politics from the Restoration until the Exclusion Crisis* (Cambridge: CUP, 1990), p. 68 quoting Kidder's *Life*, edited by A. E. Robinson (1924), p. 19.

nonconformists, could not permit the king's Indulgence to stand because of the constitutional ramifications of allowing such a suspension of parliamentary rights. It was overthrown in early 1673. Re-enforcement of the penal laws was sporadic, but the Barhams of Hackney were soon to be in trouble. Calamy recounts how

> No sooner was the King's Declaration recalled, than [Arthur Barham] was inform'd against, and his Goods were seiz'd, till he had paid a Considerable Fine. About six Weeks after, a second Warrant was issu'd out against him, though he had not then preach'd since the first: But being belov'd by his Neighbours, they gave him Notice of it, and he remov'd his Goods to London, and took Lodgings: And not long after, he was seiz'd with Apoplectick Fits, which took away his memory, and quite disabled him from farther service.[148]

2.3. Persecution Renewed

Roman Catholics were explicitly barred from any form of public service. The first Test Act was passed in 1673 – all holders of civil and military office had to take the oaths of supremacy and allegiance, sign a declaration against transubstantiation, and receive communion in the established church. This hit Dissenters, as it meant that to hold office they had to practice 'occasional conformity', an odious thing to many; but it was really aimed at Roman Catholics, which was a blow to Charles's grander strategy. It was also a blow to the Lord High Admiral and heir to the throne, James the Duke of York, for he was a covert Roman Catholic. He was forced to resign his position, his religious sympathies becoming public knowledge.

---

[148] *Calamy Revised* p. 28

The king ordered James's two daughters to be brought up as Protestants, and they were married to Protestant men as a way of appeasing the country. However, after the alleged 'Popish Plot' of 1678 sparked a wave of anti-Catholic sentiment, James was *persona non grata* in England. The Earl of Shaftesbury, who had been a member of Cromwell's Council of State and was a very experienced politician, began to agitate for James to be excluded from the line of succession to the throne, which led to a political stand-off as successive Parliaments which threatened to pass such an Exclusion Bill were dissolved. In these parliamentary battles, a good number of dissenting MPs were elected. They threw their weight behind Shaftesbury who returned the favour by pushing for comprehension and tolerance schemes to ease the burdens on dissent.

Yet with the failure of the Exclusion Bill, there came a period of so-called 'Tory Revenge'. Persecution up to this point had been sporadic but sometime fierce. 'We should be in no doubt,' writes Mark Goldie, 'about how explicitly persecution was demanded. Scarcely a tremor of embarrassment disturbed the voices of divines who called for 'a holy violence', 'a rigorous and seasonable execution of penal laws' against the 'fanatic vermin' whose conventicles 'troubled the land.'[149] Now things were intensified. In London, 'over 3800 different people were arrested and brought before the courts between 1682 and 1686 for attending Nonconformist conventicles. London Dissent was terrorised by the Hilton gang, a band of over forty thuggish

---

[149] M. Goldie, 'The Theory of Religious Intolerance in Restoration England' in O. P. Grell, J. I. Israel, and N. Tyacke (eds.), *From Persecution to Toleration: The Glorious Revolution and Religion in England* (Oxford: Clarendon Press, 1991), p. 331. The quotes are from sermons preached in the 1670s and 80s.

informers who infiltrated meetings, gathered incriminating information, participated in prosecutions, and seized Dissenters' goods by force when they failed to pay their fines.'[150]

This was a low point in the persecution years, as even the aged and fragile were abused. Slater and Watson of Crosby Hall were targeted for legal attack in 1681.[151] Arthur Barham faced '20 convictions for preaching at conventicles in his own house' in November 1682, with fines amounting to £600 imposed.[152] Thomas Woodcock was also fined £100 the same day for preaching in Hackney.[153] Richard Baxter was arrested for contravening the Five Mile Act and for preaching five sermons in 1683. His doctor testified that prison could kill him, so with the king's permission he was kept out of jail 'that I might die at home. But they Executed all their Warrants on my Books and Goods; even the bed that I lay sick on, and sold them all.'[154] The Rye House Plot to kill the king and the Duke of York convinced the government (or rather, enabled them) to continue repressing dissenters as a matter of national security. Baxter was later arrested again on scurrilous charges 'to secure the Government in evil Times', and though he was nothing but skin and bones, the infamous Judge Jeffreys abused him and recommended a flogging. Instead he was found guilty of sedition and sent to prison.

---

[150] Coffey, *Persecution and Toleration*, p. 173.
[151] Both are said in *Calamy Revised* to have been prosecuted and subpoenaed in November 1681.
[152] *Calamy Revised*, p. 28. In *Reliquiae Baxterianae*, Part III, p. 199 there are mentioned two women who made a trade of falsely informing on people and had done so 'against very many worthy persons in *Hackney* and elsewhere.'
[153] *Calamy Revised*, p. 543.
[154] See *Reliquiae Baxterianae*, Part III, p. 191. The warrants for his arrest were solicited from the Judge by 'the two Hiltons'.

2.4.   Tolerance under James II and The Glorious Revolution

When James II acceded to the throne in 1685 he was the first Roman Catholic to do so since Mary, and he shared her devotion to that church. Yet although he pushed his own religion as far and as fast as he was able, he also conceived of the plan to extend toleration to dissenters, as a way of uniting with them against the Anglicans. His *gracious declaration to all his loving subjects for liberty of conscience* in 1687 declared that although he obviously wished everyone was a Roman Catholic, 'conscience ought not to be constrained, nor people forced in matters of mere religion' since such coercion 'never obtained the end for which it was employed.' The last four reigns had sought to impose rigorous uniformity on the nation in this regard, and palpably failed – 'it is visible the success has not answered the design, and that the difficulty is invincible' declared the new king.[155] The penal laws and Test Acts were abolished, a great relief to the dissenters. And yet it was again done without consent of Parliament, though James promised to consult them on it 'when we shall think it convenient for them to meet.'[156]

It was not long before James, having alienated almost everyone, was forced to flee the country. In the wake of the harsh punishments meted out in the Bloody Assizes of Judge Jeffreys after the Monmouth rebellion many feared that Roman Catholicism would be re-established as a persecuting force in British life again. Similar accusations have, of course, been levelled at puritanism as well,[157] since to equate

---

[155] *The gracious declaration* in Cardwell, *Documentary Annals*, p. 309.
[156] *ibid.*, p. 310.
[157] Watts, *The Dissenters*, p. 221. See also C. E. Whiting, *Studies in English*

religious dissent with civil disobedience and punish it accordingly was an ancient English habit.[158] James's toleration, had it been sustainable, would have pre-empted the early nineteenth century emancipations. At this stage in our history, however, it was perhaps a step too far for the English mindset to release Roman Catholicism from all its chains.[159]

The Act of Toleration signed by James's daughter Mary and her Protestant husband William of Orange in 1689 was a step back from what James had put on the table. But unlike James's proposed solution it was not an act of arbitrary power,[160] nor was it motivated by mere short-term political expediency. After failed experiments in religious suppression on both sides, the English were ready to admit a certain degree of pluralism within a trinitarian, protestant umbrella and to reject 'the exclusivist claims of High Church Anglicans.'[161] Although it would be more than a century before protestant nonconformists gained proper civil equality, the years of persecuting them were over.

Conclusion

The period of English history from the Restoration (1660) to

Puritanism from the Restoration to the Revolution, 1660-1688 (London: Frank Cass & Co., 1968 [1931]), p. 180.

[158] See Matthews, *Calamy Revised*, p. lix.

[159] Coffey, *Persecution and Toleration*, p. 186 claims that - 'Tolerationists really did see Catholicism as a tyrannical force hell-bent on destroying Protestantism.' Even Locke thought Roman Catholics had 'an unalterable designe to destroy us.'

[160] Notwithstanding the objections of the Non-Jurors, who declined to recognise the authority of William and Mary.

[161] Bray, *Documents*, p. 571.

the Act of Toleration (1689) is a formative one in our religious history. Conformity and nonconformity, rather than being parties vying for influence within the same established church, became the separate institutions we know today as the Church of England and the 'Free Churches', although they would continue to influence each other at many different levels. The debates and debacles of these years taught the English church the important fundamental truth, that in matters of religion 'God alone is Lord of the conscience' and it ought not to be compelled by 'the doctrines and commandments of men'.[162] As Martin Luther had discovered at the start of the Reformation, it was neither right nor safe to go against conscience; it was now also clear that coercing another's was a dangerous game.

Yet some disciplinary and doctrinal boundaries always need to be drawn in the Church; toleration cannot lightly be granted to forces which would undermine the basis of tolerance itself. The Church of England has never been infinitely elastic in its doctrinal inclusiveness, a 'melting pot' for an unlimited variety of Christian traditions, as some assert today. It was certainly not that in this key foundational year of 1662! As the church of the seventeenth century was wary of a too ready accommodation with reactionary Roman Catholicism, so the twenty-first century should be chary of the 'affirming' yet all too authoritarian inclusivity sought by its liberal extremists. Whether an established church controlled by such people will refurbish its former reputation as an agent of persecution against reformed Christianity is unclear, though there are ominous signs that it could drift into collaboration with the state in pursuit of an amoral,

---

[162] Westminster Confession of Faith XX.ii.

secularist agenda.

1662 was not, as Lloyd-Jones asserted, the year that '[t]he hope of the Puritans was finally dashed to the ground ... their final defeat, and the exploding of all their longings.'[163] It was, to be sure, a defeat for one generation; but one from which a form of puritan piety and reforming zeal has in a sense recovered in the subsequent 300 years. The resurrection of evangelicalism, especially 'classic' evangelicalism, within the Church of England in recent years demonstrates that there may still be some hope of reforming the national church. The continued presence of reformed ministers and laypeople within the denomination's ranks is an essential prophylactic against further degradation of its doctrinal quality. It would be a tragedy, therefore, if another issue of conscience such as (for instance) an attempt to compel all ministers to accept the authority of women bishops, were to force such people out in a manner reminiscent of 1662.

Needless to say, the established church is not the same as it was in the mid-seventeenth century. The Church of England has now incorporated some of the key features of Usher's synodical system into its form of government,[164] although it lacks bishops with the same reformed theology and understanding of episcopacy as Usher to run it. The issue, as we noted above (footnote 90), is that evangelical

---

[163] D. M. Lloyd-Jones, *The Puritans: Their Origins and Successors* (Edinburgh: Banner of Truth, 1987), p. 58.
[164] On which see footnote 35 above. A key study of this is W. Benn, *Usher on Bishops: A Reforming Ecclesiology* (St Antholin's Lectureship Charity Lecture, 2002), p. 24 of which rightly points out that '[Usher's] synodical vision is only now being implemented in the church, but our outworking lacks his concern for godly discipline and gospel rule in our church.'

churches must enthusiastically populate the system of synods and councils with men and women of ability and reliability in order to make it work for them effectively. The gospel must be applied in every area of life, not least in ecclesiastical politics, with rigor and passion. A failure to engage with the system by maximising the advantage evangelical churches often have in terms of human resources is to play into liberal or Anglo-Catholic hands.

Happily, the Church of England also no longer insists on 'unfeigned consent and assent' to absolutely everything in its liturgy and Articles.[165] Evangelicals may (and should) be more comfortable with the 1552 Prayer Book as opposed to the 1662 revision, but today the Prayer Book is only one of the often bewildering array of liturgical options. There is flexibility, perhaps too much flexibility doctrinally, in the recent *Common Worship*, and local variations in style (of which evangelicals are often enthusiastic supporters) often go unchallenged even while the official position of the denomination is occasionally far too rigid, as with the laws regarding robes for instance. Thankfully, common sense usually prevails over legalistic enforcement on such issues.

Subscription to the Articles has been weakened since the 1960s,[166] with even evangelical theological students not in favour of retaining a tight subscription.[167] All the same,

---

[165] Canon B5, for instance, allows a certain liturgical discretion to ministers, who can use variations in wording providing they are 'reverent and seemly and shall be neither contrary to, nor indicative of any departure from, the doctrine of the Church of England in any essential matter.'

[166] See the official report which led to the changes, *Subscription and Assent to the Thirty-nine Articles: A Report of the Archbishops' Commission on Christian Doctrine* (London: SPCK, 1968).

[167] According to a survey done by Michael Green (an evangelical member of the Doctrine Commission at the time, along with J. I. Packer) on which see his

ordinands must affirm their loyalty to an inheritance of faith which includes the Articles alongside the catholic creeds but which affirms above all the supremacy of Scripture: 'I, A. B., ... declare my belief in the faith which is revealed in the Holy Scriptures.'[168] Article 6 still declares that, 'Holy Scripture containeth all things necessary to salvation: so that whatsoever is not read therein, nor may be proved thereby, is not to be required of any man, that it should be believed an article of the Faith, or be thought requisite to salvation.' That this official line on 'the faith uniquely revealed in the Holy Scriptures' is not more often heard in public or applied in practice reflects badly not only on those who declare their assent to it at their ordination, but also on those in the pews who are often complicit in the intrusion of other 'authorities' into the pastoral ministry. It would be better if erroneous doctrine outside the pale of orthodoxy was easier to banish from our pulpits, but it is rarely the fault of bishops alone that false teaching is propagated in the church.

Although the established church persists in refusing to recognise non-episcopal ordination and confirmation, the old seventeenth century debates over church government or

---

Adventure of Faith: Reflections on Fifty Years of Christian Service (Harrow: Zondervan, 2001), pp. 295-298. Podmore demonstrates in *Aspects of Anglican Identity*, p. 57 that 'the Declaration of Assent [in today's Canon Law] can be said to be ... a fruit of the much-maligned synodical process.'

[168] The Declaration of Assent made by every deacon, presbyter, bishop, and archbishop in the Church of England. The preface to this declares that the Church of England 'professes the faith uniquely revealed in the Holy Scriptures.' Canon A5 also declares that 'The doctrine of the Church of England is grounded in the Holy Scriptures, and in such teachings of the ancient Fathers and Councils of the Church as are agreeable to the said Scriptures. In particular such doctrine is to be found in the Thirty-nine Articles of Religion, *The Book of Common Prayer*, and the Ordinal'. Thus the hierarchy of authorities in official Anglicanism always has Scripture as supreme.

ceremonial may not divide as they once did. Today it is the doctrine of creation (with its entailments in the areas of sexual morality, the sacredness of life, the sanctity of marriage, and relationships between the genders) which has a good claim to be the new frontline in dispute. Those who dissent from the prevailing attitude of the powerful few at the heart of government on such issues may yet find themselves in an unenviable position similar to that of the puritans of the Restoration era. Yet this should be interpreted not as a reason to despair but as an urgent call to continue reform of the denomination. It has an honoured history in the evangelisation and edification of the nation, and must be strengthened against such destructive tides. It would be foolish to abandon a leaky but serviceable vessel, and criminally negligent to find oneself thrown overboard merely for lack of proper attention to what was going on.

On the dissenting side, 1662 is remembered as the year the so-called 'national' church became a sect, excluding and then persecuting fellow Christians who were restrained from hearing the word or celebrating the sacraments elsewhere. Many within its bounds retained a great sympathy for puritan theology and practice, which would later prove to be a force for the church's renewal and revival. Conversely, as Carl Trueman has written,

> The Great Ejection of 1662 effectively removed from the Church, and thus from the intellectual establishment, the vast majority of those ministers committed to a more thoroughly Reformed faith; it therefore surrendered both the Church, and, as a result, the academy to a group whose theological concerns were generally more latitudinarian. In the twentieth century the Anglican monopoly of higher education has gone, but Anglicans have continued to set much of the scholarly agenda within university theology departments, and so have determined that the subjects

studied reflect their own ecclesiastical concerns.[169]

This in turn had dramatic theological effects on the dissenting community. A stress on 'the Bible alone' to the exclusion of systematic and historical theology led to a great many Presbyterian, Congregational, and Baptist churches being fatally infected with Unitarianism in the century after the Ejection.[170] This was due in no small part to greatly weakened (sometimes determinedly non-existent) ministerial subscription to articles of faith, and the disuse of the ancient creeds in public worship. The dominance of the academy by persecuting Anglicans and the linking of the idea of subscription with their despised Prayer Book and Articles may have been partly responsible for some of this doctrinal drift. Yet what is certain is that many dissenting congregations were lost to orthodox trinitarian Christianity as a result.

Whether the Great Ejection and Great Persecution were a tragedy for the gospel itself, as many thought at the time, is less certain in the long run. As Thomas Hardcastle, the Pastor of the Broadmead Baptists 'seven times imprisoned for Christ and a good conscience' wisely admonished his flock:

> It has been our great error that we have not trusted in the power of God. We have reasoned about the worst that men can do, but have not believed the best that God can do ... We are sowing for posterity; the generation coming on will have the good fruit of this present persecution.[171]

---

[169] C. Trueman, *The Claims of Truth: John Owen's Trinitarian Theology* (Carlisle: Paternoster, 1998), p. 2.
[170] See Watts, *The Dissenters,* pp. 371-382.
[171] *ibid.,* p. 242.

Much good fruit survived. The loss of the dissenters was a tragedy for the national church, but nonconformity blossomed to some extent under persecution. Major literary works such as Milton's *Paradise Lost,* Bunyan's *Pilgrim's Progress,* and John Owen's monumental Hebrews commentary were all written during the persecution years. A vibrant gospel witness freed from the shackles of the establishment survived. Theological distinctives on secondary issues such as credobaptism, which were unacceptable within the established church, were able later to flourish and grow outside the traditional boundaries, and many were brought to faith both here and abroad through Baptist preachers. To some degree the wheat was sorted from the chaff within nonconformity too since persecution can be a refining experience, particularly when a more comfortable way of being a Christian is on offer for the price of just a few compromises.

There is also fruit for today. There remains still much to be savoured in reflecting on the example of faith in the men and women of that former heroic age. For them doctrine mattered, and the truth was worth fighting, dying, and being ejected for. There should perhaps have been much greater unity in practice between those Anglicans, Presbyterians, Independents, and Baptists who agreed on the foundational tenets of the faith. By failing to work together more effectively they gave a huge boost not just to the Laudians but also to those who held the gospel itself in contempt. It is for this present generation to ensure that all these lessons of history are not ignored.

FOR FURTHER READING

Primary Sources

R. Baxter, *The Autobiography of Richard Baxter* abridged by J. M. Lloyd Thomas, edited with an introduction by N. H. Keeble (London : J. M. Dent & Sons, 1985)

C. Buchanan, *The Savoy Conference Revisited: the proceedings taken from the Grand Debate of 1661 and the works of Richard Baxter* (Cambridge: Grove Books, 2002)

G. Gould, *Documents Relating to the Settlement of the Church of England by the Act of Uniformity of 1662* (London: W. Kent & Co, 1862)

A. G. Matthews, *Calamy Revised: Being a Revision of Edmund Calamy's Account of the Ministers and Others Ejected and Silenced, 1660-1662* (Oxford: Clarendon Press,1988 [1934])

I. Murray (ed.), *Sermons of the Great Ejection* (Edinburgh: Banner of Truth, 1962)

Secondary Sources

R. S. Bosher, *The Making of the Restoration Settlement: The Influence of the Laudians 1649-1662* (London: Dacre Press, 1951)

J. Coffey, *Persecution and Toleration in Protestant England, 1558-1689* (London: Longman, 2000)

G. R. Cragg, *Puritanism in the Period of the Great Persecution 1660-1688* (Cambridge: CUP, 1957)

I. M. Green, *The Re-Establishment of the Church of England 1660-1663* (Oxford, OUP, 1978)

R. Hutton, *The Restoration: A Political and Religious History of England and Wales 1658-1667* (Oxford: Clarendon Press, 1985)

G. F. Nuttall and O. Chadwick (eds.), *From Uniformity to Unity 1662-1962* (London: SPCK, 1962)

P. Seaward, *The Cavalier Parliament and the Reconstruction of the Old Regime, 1661-1667* (Cambridge: CUP, 1989)

M. Watts, *The Dissenters: From the Reformation to the French Revolution* (Oxford: Clarendon Press, 1978)

Latimer Studies